Cooking for Kids

RECIPES KIDS LOVE

Publications International, Ltd.

Favorite Brand Name Recipes at www.fbnr.com

Pictured on the front cover: Birthday Extravaganza *(page 82).*
Pictured on the back cover *(top to bottom):* Bamboozlers *(page 72)* and Dino-Mite Dinosaurs *(page 46).*

ISBN: 1-4127-2030-3

Manufactured in China.

8 7 6 5 4 3 2 1

Microwave Cooking: Microwave ovens vary in wattage. Use the cooking times as guidelines and check for doneness before adding more time.

Preparation/Cooking Times: Preparation times are based on the approximate amount of time required to assemble the recipe before cooking, baking, chilling or serving. These times include preparation steps such as measuring, chopping and mixing. The fact that some preparations and cooking can be done simultaneously is taken into account. Preparation of optional ingredients and serving suggestions is not included.

TABLE OF CONTENTS

SNACK ATTACK

Señor Nacho Dip

Makes 4 servings

   4 ounces fat-free cream cheese
   ½ cup (2 ounces) shredded Cheddar cheese
   ¼ cup mild or medium chunky salsa
   2 teaspoons low-fat (2%) milk
   **4 ounces baked tortilla chips or assorted fresh vegetable
      dippers**

1. Combine cream cheese and Cheddar cheese in small saucepan; stir over low heat until melted. Stir in salsa and milk; heat thoroughly, stirring occasionally.

2. Transfer dip to small serving bowl. Serve with tortilla chips. Garnish with hot peppers and cilantro, if desired.

Olé Dip: Substitute reduced-fat Monterey Jack cheese or taco cheese for Cheddar cheese.

Spicy Mustard Dip: Omit tortilla chips. Substitute 2 teaspoons spicy brown or honey mustard for salsa. Serve with fresh vegetable dippers or pretzels.

Señor Nacho Dip

Pizza Fondue

Makes 20 to 25 appetizer servings

- ½ pound bulk Italian sausage
- 1 cup chopped onion
- 2 jars (26 ounces each) meatless pasta sauce
- 4 ounces thinly sliced ham, finely chopped
- 1 package (3 ounces) sliced pepperoni, finely chopped
- ¼ teaspoon red pepper flakes
- 1 pound mozzarella cheese, cut into ¾-inch cubes
- 1 loaf Italian or French bread, cut into 1-inch cubes

Slow Cooker Directions

1. Cook sausage and onion in large skillet until sausage is browned. Drain off fat.

2. Transfer sausage mixture to slow cooker. Stir in pasta sauce, ham, pepperoni and pepper flakes. Cover; cook on LOW 3 to 4 hours.

3. Serve sauce with cheese cubes, bread cubes and fondue forks.

Prep Time: *15 minutes*
Cook Time: *3 to 4 hours*

Sugar-and-Spice Twists

Makes 6 servings

- 1 tablespoon sugar
- ¼ teaspoon ground cinnamon
- 1 package (6) refrigerated breadsticks

1. Preheat oven to 350°F. Lightly grease baking sheet or line with parchment paper.

2. Stir together sugar and cinnamon. Place in shallow dish or plate.

3. Open package of breadsticks. Divide into 6 portions. Roll each portion into 12-inch rope. Roll in sugar mixture. Twist into pretzel shape. Place on prepared baking sheet. Bake 15 to 18 minutes or until lightly browned. Remove from baking sheet. Cool 5 minutes. Serve warm.

Tip: Use colored sugar sprinkles in place of the sugar in this recipe for a fun 'twist' of color that's perfect for holidays, birthdays or simply everyday celebrations.

Pizza Fondue

Confetti Tuna in Celery Sticks

Makes 10 to 12 servings

- 1 (3-ounce) pouch of STARKIST® Premium Albacore or Chunk Light Tuna
- ½ cup shredded red or green cabbage
- ½ cup shredded carrot
- ¼ cup shredded yellow squash or zucchini
- 3 tablespoons reduced-calorie cream cheese, softened
- 1 tablespoon plain low-fat yogurt
- ½ teaspoon dried basil, crushed
- Salt and pepper to taste
- 10 to 12 (4-inch) celery sticks, with leaves if desired

1. In a small bowl toss together tuna, cabbage, carrot and squash.

2. Stir in cream cheese, yogurt and basil. Add salt and pepper to taste.

3. With small spatula spread mixture evenly into celery sticks.

Prep Time: *20 minutes*

Cinnamon Apple Chips

Makes about 40 chips

- 2 cups unsweetened apple juice
- 1 cinnamon stick
- 2 Washington Red Delicious apples

1. In large skillet or saucepan, combine apple juice and cinnamon stick; bring to a low boil while preparing apples.

2. With paring knife, slice off ½ inch from tops and bottoms of apples and discard (or eat). Stand apples on either cut end; cut crosswise into ⅛-inch-thick slices, rotating apple as necessary to cut even slices.

3. Drop slices into boiling juice; cook 4 to 5 minutes or until slices appear translucent and lightly golden. Meanwhile, preheat oven to 250°F.

4. With slotted spatula, remove apple slices from juice and pat dry. Arrange slices on wire racks, being sure none overlap. Place racks on middle shelf in oven; bake 30 to 40 minutes until slices are lightly browned and almost dry to touch. Let chips cool on racks completely before storing in airtight container.

Tip: There is no need to core apples because boiling in juice for several minutes softens core and removes seeds.

*Favorite recipe from **Washington Apple Commission***

Confetti Tuna in Celery Sticks

Banana Freezer Pops

Makes 8 servings

2 ripe medium bananas
1 can (6 ounces) frozen orange juice concentrate, thawed
¼ cup water
1 tablespoon honey
1 teaspoon vanilla
8 (3-ounce) paper or plastic cups
8 wooden sticks

1. Peel bananas; break into chunks. Place in food processor or blender container.

2. Add orange juice concentrate, water, honey and vanilla; process until smooth.

3. Pour banana mixture evenly into cups. Cover top of each cup with small piece of aluminum foil. Insert wooden stick through center of foil into banana mixture.

4. Place cups on tray; freeze until firm, about 3 hours. To serve, remove foil; tear off paper cups (or slide out of plastic cups).

Peppy Purple Pops: Omit honey and vanilla. Substitute grape juice concentrate for orange juice concentrate.

Frozen Banana Shakes: Increase water to 1½ cups. Prepare fruit mixture as directed. Add 4 ice cubes; process on high speed until mixture is thick and creamy. Makes 3 servings.

Banana Freezer Pops

Tortellini Teasers

Makes 6 servings

Zesty Tomato Sauce (recipe follows)
½ (9-ounce) package refrigerated cheese tortellini
1 large red or green bell pepper, cut into 1-inch pieces
2 medium carrots, peeled and sliced ½ inch thick
1 medium zucchini, sliced ½ inch thick
12 medium fresh mushrooms
12 cherry tomatoes

1. Prepare Zesty Tomato Sauce; keep warm.

2. Cook tortellini according to package directions; drain.

3. Alternate 1 tortellini and 2 to 3 vegetable pieces on long frilled toothpicks or wooden skewers. Serve as dippers with tomato sauce.

Zesty Tomato Sauce

1 can (15 ounces) tomato purée
2 tablespoons finely chopped onion
2 tablespoons chopped fresh parsley
1 teaspoon dried oregano leaves
¼ teaspoon dried thyme leaves
¼ teaspoon salt
⅛ teaspoon black pepper

Combine tomato purée, onion, parsley, oregano and thyme in small saucepan. Heat thoroughly, stirring occasionally. Stir in salt and pepper. Garnish with carrot curl, if desired.

Tortellini Teasers

Dipped, Drizzled & Decorated Pretzels

Makes about 2 dozen pretzels

1 bag chocolate or flavored chips (choose semisweet, bittersweet, milk chocolate, green mint, white chocolate, butterscotch, peanut butter or a combination)
1 bag pretzel rods
Assorted toppings: jimmies, sprinkles, chopped nuts, coconut, toasted coconut, cookie crumbs, colored sugars (optional)

Microwave Directions

1. Place chips in microwavable bowl. (Be sure bowl and utensils are completely dry.) Cover with plastic wrap and turn back one corner to vent. Microwave at HIGH 1 minute; stir. Return to microwave and continue cooking in 30-second intervals until chips are completely melted. Check and stir frequently.

2. Dip one half of each pretzel rod into melted chocolate and decorate, if desired. Roll coated end of several pretzels in toppings. Drizzle others with contrasting color/flavor melted chips. (Drizzle melted chocolate out of spoon while rotating pretzel, to get even coverage.)

3. Place decorated pretzels on cooling rack; set over baking sheet lined with waxed-paper. Let coating harden completely. Do not refrigerate.

Dipped, Drizzled & Decorated Pretzels

Taco Popcorn Olé

Makes 6 (1½-cup) servings

9 cups air-popped popcorn
   Butter-flavored cooking spray
1 teaspoon chili powder
½ teaspoon salt
½ teaspoon garlic powder
⅛ teaspoon ground red pepper (optional)

1. Preheat oven to 350°F. Line 15×10-inch jelly-roll pan with foil.

2. Place popcorn in single layer in prepared pan. Coat lightly with cooking spray.

3. Combine chili powder, salt, garlic powder and red pepper, if desired, in small bowl; sprinkle over popcorn. Mix lightly to coat evenly.

4. Bake 5 minutes or until hot, stirring gently after 3 minutes. Spread mixture in single layer on large sheet of foil to cool.

Tip: Store popcorn mixture in tightly covered container at room temperature up to 4 days.

Quick S'Mores

Makes 1 serving

1 whole graham cracker
1 large marshmallow
1 teaspoon hot fudge sauce

1. Break graham cracker in half crosswise. Place one half on small paper plate or microwavable plate; top with marshmallow.

2. Spread remaining ½ of cracker with fudge sauce.

3. Place cracker with marshmallow in microwave. Microwave at HIGH 12 to 14 seconds or until marshmallow puffs up. Immediately place remaining cracker, fudge side down, over marshmallow. Press crackers gently to even out marshmallow layer. Cool completely.

Cook's Tip: S'mores can be made the night before and wrapped in plastic wrap or sealed in a small plastic food storage bag. Store at room temperature until ready to pack in your child's lunch box the next morning.

Taco Popcorn Olé

WHAT'S FOR LUNCH?

Buffalo-Style Wraps

Makes 4 servings

  ⅔ cup **Frank's®** **RedHot®** Original Cayenne Pepper Sauce, divided
  4 boneless skinless chicken breast halves
  ¼ cup blue cheese salad dressing
  1 cup shredded lettuce
  1 cup (4 ounces) shredded Monterey Jack cheese
  4 (10-inch) flour tortillas, heated

1. Combine ⅓ cup **Frank's RedHot** Sauce and *1 tablespoon oil* in resealable plastic food storage bag. Add chicken. Seal bag; toss to coat evenly. Marinate in refrigerator 30 minutes or overnight.

2. Broil or grill chicken 10 to 15 minutes or until no longer pink in center. Slice chicken into long thin strips. In bowl, toss chicken with remaining ⅓ cup **Frank's RedHot** Sauce and dressing.

3. Arrange chicken, lettuce and cheese down center of tortillas, dividing evenly. Fold bottom third of each tortilla over filling; fold sides towards center. Tightly roll up to secure filling. Cut in half to serve.

Prep Time: *10 minutes*
Cook Time: *10 minutes*

Buffalo-Style Wrap

Little Piggy Pies

Makes 5 servings

2 cups frozen mixed soup vegetables (such as carrots, potatoes, peas, celery, green beans, corn and onions)
1 (10¾-ounce) can reduced-fat condensed cream of chicken soup, undiluted
8 ounces chopped cooked chicken
⅓ cup plain low-fat yogurt
⅓ cup water
½ teaspoon dried thyme leaves
¼ teaspoon poultry seasoning or ground sage
⅛ teaspoon garlic powder
1 (7½-ounce) tube (10) refrigerated buttermilk biscuits

1. Preheat oven to 400°F.

2. Remove 10 green peas from frozen mixed vegetables. Stir together remaining frozen vegetables, soup, chicken, yogurt, water, thyme, poultry seasoning and garlic powder in medium saucepan. Bring to a boil, stirring frequently. Cover; keep warm.

3. Press five biscuits into 3-inch circles. Cut each remaining biscuit into eight wedges. Place two wedges on top of each circle; fold points down to form ears. Roll one wedge into small ball; place in center of each circle to form pig's snout. Use tip of spoon handle to make indents in snout for nostrils. Place 2 reserved green peas on each circle for eyes.

4. Spoon hot chicken mixture into 5 (10-ounce) custard cups. Place one biscuit "pig" on top of each. Place remaining biscuit wedges around each "pig" on top of chicken mixture, twisting one wedge "tail" for each. Bake 9 to 11 minutes or until biscuits are golden.

Prep Time: *10 minutes*
Bake Time: *11 minutes*

Little Piggy Pie

Turkey and Macaroni

Makes 4 to 6 servings

- 1 teaspoon vegetable oil
- 1½ pounds ground turkey
- 2 cans (10¾ ounces each) condensed tomato soup, undiluted
- 2 cups uncooked macaroni, cooked and drained
- 1 can (16 ounces) corn, drained
- ½ cup chopped onion
- 1 can (4 ounces) sliced mushrooms, drained
- 2 tablespoons ketchup
- 1 tablespoon mustard
- Salt and black pepper to taste

Slow Cooker Directions

Heat oil in medium skillet; cook turkey until browned. Transfer mixture to slow cooker. Add remaining ingredients to slow cooker. Stir to blend. Cover and cook on LOW 7 to 9 hours or on HIGH 3 to 4 hours.

Finger Licking Chicken Salad

Makes 1 serving

- ½ cup diced roasted skinless chicken breast
- ½ rib celery, cut into 1-inch pieces
- ¼ cup drained mandarin orange segments
- ¼ cup red seedless grapes
- 2 tablespoons fat-free sugar-free lemon yogurt
- 1 tablespoon reduced-fat mayonnaise
- ¼ teaspoon reduced-sodium soy sauce
- ⅛ teaspoon pumpkin pie spice or cinnamon

1. Toss together chicken, celery, oranges and grapes. Place in covered plastic container.

2. For dipping sauce, stir together yogurt, mayonnaise, soy sauce and pumpkin pie spice.

3. Pack chicken mixture and dipping sauce in insulated bag with ice pack. To serve, dip chicken mixture into dipping sauce.

Variation: Alternately thread the chicken, celery, oranges and grapes on wooden skewers for a different way to serve this recipe.

Turkey and Macaroni

Bologna "Happy Faces"

Makes 4 open-faced sandwiches

4 slices whole wheat or rye bread
1 cup prepared oil and vinegar based coleslaw
8 ounces HEBREW NATIONAL® Sliced Lean Beef Bologna or
  Lean Beef Salami
4 large pimiento-stuffed green olives
  HEBREW NATIONAL® Deli Mustard

For each sandwich, spread 1 bread slice with 3 tablespoons coleslaw; top with 5 slices bologna. Cut olives in half crosswise; place over bologna for "eyes." Draw smiley "mouth" with mustard. Drop 1 tablespoon coleslaw at top of face for "hair."

Pizza Turnovers

Makes 6 servings

5 ounces reduced-fat Italian bulk turkey sausage (mild)
½ cup pizza sauce
1 (10-ounce) package refrigerated pizza dough
⅓ cup shredded reduced-fat Italian cheese blend

1. Preheat oven to 425°F. Cook sausage in nonstick saucepan until browned, stirring with spoon to break up meat. Drain off fat. Stir in pizza sauce. Cook until hot.

2. Spray baking sheet with nonstick olive oil cooking spray. Unroll pizza dough onto baking sheet. Pat into 12×8-inch rectangle. Cut into six 4×4-inch squares. Divide sausage mixture evenly among squares. Sprinkle with cheese. Lift one corner of each square and fold dough over filling to opposite corner, making a triangle. Press edges with tines of fork to seal.

3. Bake 11 to 13 minutes or until golden brown. Serve immediately or follow directions for freezing and reheating.

Note: To freeze turnovers, remove to wire rack to cool 30 minutes. Individually wrap in plastic wrap, place in freezer container or plastic freezer bag and freeze. To reheat turnovers, preheat oven to 400°F. Unwrap turnovers. Place in ungreased baking pan. Cover loosely with foil. Bake 18 to 22 minutes or until hot. Or, place one turnover on a paper-towel-lined microwavable plate. Heat on DEFROST (30% power) 3 to 3½ minutes or until hot, turning once.

Bologna "Happy Faces"

Kid's Choice Meatballs

Makes 6 to 8 servings (about 48 meatballs)

1½ pounds ground beef
¼ cup dry seasoned bread crumbs
¼ cup grated Parmesan cheese
3 tablespoons *French's®* Worcestershire Sauce
1 egg
2 jars (14 ounces each) spaghetti sauce

1. Preheat oven to 425°F. In bowl, gently mix beef, bread crumbs, cheese, Worcestershire and egg. Shape into 1-inch meatballs. Place on rack in roasting pan. Bake 15 minutes or until cooked.

2. In large saucepan, combine meatballs and spaghetti sauce. Cook until heated through. Serve over cooked pasta.

Prep Time: *10 minutes*
Cook Time: *20 minutes*

Quick Meatball Tip: On waxed paper, pat meat mixture into 8×6×1-inch rectangle. With knife, cut crosswise and lengthwise into 1-inch rows. Roll each small square into a ball.

Tacos Olé

Makes 4 servings

1 pound ground beef or turkey
1 cup salsa
¼ cup *Frank's® RedHot®* Original Cayenne Pepper Sauce
2 teaspoons chili powder
8 taco shells, heated
   Garnish: chopped tomatoes, shredded lettuce, sliced olives, sour cream, shredded cheese

1. Cook beef in skillet over medium-high heat 5 minutes or until browned, stirring to separate meat; drain. Stir in salsa, **Frank's RedHot** Sauce and chili powder. Heat to boiling. Reduce heat to medium-low. Cook 5 minutes, stirring often.

2. To serve, spoon meat mixture into taco shells. Splash on more **Frank's RedHot** Sauce to taste. Garnish as desired.

Prep Time: *5 minutes*
Cook Time: *10 minutes*

Kid's Choice Meatballs

Crunchy Turkey Pita Pockets

Makes 2 servings

- 1 cup diced cooked turkey or chicken breast or reduced-sodium deli turkey breast
- ½ cup packaged cole slaw mix
- ½ cup dried cranberries
- ¼ cup shredded carrots
- 2 tablespoons reduced-fat or fat-free mayonnaise
- 1 tablespoon honey mustard
- 2 whole wheat pita breads

1. Combine turkey, cole slaw mix, cranberries, carrots, mayonnaise and mustard in small bowl; mix well.

2. Cut pita breads in half; fill with turkey mixture.

Chunky Chicken and Vegetable Soup

Makes 4 servings

- 1 tablespoon vegetable oil
- 1 boneless skinless chicken breast (4 ounces), diced
- ½ cup chopped green bell pepper
- ½ cup thinly sliced celery
- 2 green onions, sliced
- 2 cans (14½ ounces each) chicken broth
- 1 cup water
- ½ cup sliced carrots
- 2 tablespoons cream
- 1 tablespoon finely chopped parsley
- ¼ teaspoon dried thyme leaves
- ⅛ teaspoon black pepper

1. Heat oil in large saucepan over medium heat. Add chicken; cook and stir 4 to 5 minutes or until no longer pink. Add bell pepper, celery and onions. Cook and stir 7 minutes or until vegetables are tender.

2. Add broth, water, carrots, cream, parsley, thyme and black pepper. Simmer 10 minutes or until carrots are tender.

Crunchy Turkey Pita Pockets

Ham & Cheese Shells & Trees

Makes 4 servings

> 2 tablespoons margarine or butter
> 1 (6.2-ounce) package PASTA RONI® Shells & White Cheddar
> 2 cups fresh or frozen chopped broccoli
> ⅔ cup milk
> 1½ cups ham or cooked turkey, cut into thin strips
> (about 6 ounces)

1. In large saucepan, bring 2 cups water and margarine to a boil.

2. Stir in pasta. Reduce heat to medium. Gently boil, uncovered, 6 minutes, stirring occasionally. Stir in broccoli; return to a boil. Boil 6 to 8 minutes or until most of water is absorbed.

3. Stir in milk, ham and Special Seasonings. Return to a boil; boil 1 to 2 minutes or until pasta is tender. Let stand 5 minutes before serving.

Prep Time: *5 minutes*
Cook Time: *20 minutes*

Tip: No leftovers? Ask the deli to slice a ½-inch-thick piece of ham or turkey.

Dizzy Dogs

Makes 8 hot dogs

> 1 package (8 breadsticks) refrigerated breadsticks
> 1 package (16 ounces) hot dogs
> 1 egg white
> Sesame and/or poppy seeds
> Mustard, ketchup and barbecue sauce (optional)

1. Preheat oven to 375°F.

2. Using 1 breadstick for each, wrap hot dogs with dough in spiral pattern. Brush breadstick dough with egg white and sprinkle with sesame and/or poppy seeds. Place on *ungreased* baking sheet.

3. Bake 12 to 15 minutes or until light golden brown. Serve with condiments for dipping, if desired.

Ham & Cheese Shells & Trees

Chicken nuggets with Barbecue Dipping Sauce

Makes 8 servings

- **1 pound boneless skinless chicken breasts**
- **¼ cup all-purpose flour**
- **¼ teaspoon salt**
- **¼ teaspoon black pepper**
- **2 cups crushed reduced-fat baked cheese crackers**
- **1 teaspoon dried oregano leaves**
- **1 egg white**
- **1 tablespoon water**
- **3 tablespoons barbecue sauce**
- **2 tablespoons no-sugar-added peach or apricot jam**

1. Preheat oven to 400°F. Rinse chicken. Pat dry with paper towels. Cut into 1-inch chunks.

2. Place flour, salt and pepper in resealable plastic food storage bag. Combine cracker crumbs and oregano in shallow bowl. Whisk together egg white and water in small bowl.

3. Place 6 or 8 chicken pieces in bag with flour mixture; seal bag. Shake bag until chicken is well coated. Remove chicken from bag, shaking off excess flour. Dip chicken pieces into egg white mixture, coating all sides. Roll in crumb mixture. Place in shallow baking pan. Repeat with remaining chicken pieces. Bake 10 to 13 minutes or until golden brown.

4. Meanwhile, stir together barbecue sauce and jam in small saucepan. Cook and stir over low heat until heated through. (If freezing nuggets, do not prepare dipping sauce at this time.) Serve chicken nuggets with dipping sauce or follow directions for freezing and reheating.

Note: To freeze chicken nuggets, cool 5 minutes on baking sheet. Wrap chicken in plastic wrap, making packages of 4 to 5 nuggets each. Place packages in freezer container or plastic freezer bag. Freeze.

Note: To reheat nuggets, preheat oven to 325°F. Unwrap nuggets. Place nuggets on ungreased baking sheet. Bake 13 to 15 minutes or until hot. Or, place 4 to 5 nuggets on microwavable plate. Heat on DEFROST (30% power) for 2½ to 3½ minutes or until hot, turning once. For each serving, stir together about 1½ teaspoons barbecue sauce and ½ teaspoon jam in small microwavable dish. Heat on HIGH 10 to 15 seconds or until hot.

Chicken Nuggets with Barbecue Dipping Sauce

COOKIE CRAVINGS

Sandwich Cookies

Makes about 20 to 24 sandwich cookies

1 package (20 ounces) refrigerated cookie dough, any flavor
All-purpose flour (optional)
Any combination of colored frostings, peanut butter or assorted ice creams for filling
Colored sprinkles, chocolate-covered raisins, miniature candy-coated chocolate pieces and other assorted small candies for decoration

1. Preheat oven to 350°F. Grease cookie sheets.

2. Remove dough from wrapper according to package directions. Cut dough into 4 equal sections. Reserve 1 section; refrigerate remaining 3 sections.

3. Roll reserved dough to ¼-inch thickness. Sprinkle with flour to minimize sticking, if necessary.

4. Cut out cookies using ¾-inch round or fluted cookie cutter. Transfer cookies to prepared cookie sheets, placing about 2 inches apart. Repeat steps with remaining dough.

5. Bake 8 to 11 minutes or until edges are lightly browned. Remove to wire racks; cool completely.

6. To make sandwich, spread about 1 tablespoon desired filling on flat side of 1 cookie to within ¼ inch of edge. Top with second cookie, pressing gently. Roll side of sandwich in desired decorations. Repeat with remaining cookies.

Sandwich Cookies

Hershey's Milk Chocolate Chip Giant Cookies

Makes about 12 to 16 servings

6 tablespoons butter, softened
½ cup granulated sugar
¼ cup packed light brown sugar
½ teaspoon vanilla extract
1 egg
1 cup all-purpose flour
½ teaspoon baking soda
2 cups (11½-ounce package) HERSHEY'S Milk Chocolate Chips
Frosting (optional)
Ice cream (optional)

1. Heat oven to 350°F. Line two 9-inch round baking pans with foil, extending foil over edges of pans.

2. Beat butter, granulated sugar, brown sugar and vanilla until fluffy. Add egg; beat well. Stir together flour and baking soda; gradually add to butter mixture, beating until well blended. Stir in milk chocolate chips. Spread one half of batter into each prepared pan, spreading to 1 inch from edge. (Cookies will spread to edge when baking.)

3. Bake 18 to 22 minutes or until lightly browned. Cool completely; carefully lift cookies from pans and remove foil. Frost, if desired. Cut each cookie into wedges; serve topped with scoop of ice cream, if desired.

TIP: Bake cookies on the middle rack of the oven, one pan at a time. Uneven browning can occur if baking on more than one rack at the same time.

Hershey's Milk Chocolate Chip Giant Cookie

Butterfly Cookies

Makes about 20 to 22 cookies

2¼ cups all-purpose flour
¼ teaspoon salt
1 cup sugar
¾ cup (1½ sticks) butter, softened
1 egg
1 teaspoon vanilla
1 teaspoon almond extract
White frosting, assorted food colorings, colored sugars, assorted small decors, gummy fruit and hard candies for decoration

1. Combine flour and salt in medium bowl; set aside.

2. Beat sugar and butter in large bowl at medium speed of electric mixer until fluffy. Beat in egg, vanilla and almond extract. Gradually add flour mixture. Beat at low speed until well blended. Divide dough in half. Cover; refrigerate 30 minutes or until firm.

3. Preheat oven to 350°F. Grease cookie sheets. Roll half of dough on lightly floured surface to ¼-inch thickness. Cut out cookies using butterfly cookie cutters. Repeat with remaining dough.

4. Bake 12 to 15 minutes or until edges are lightly browned. Remove to wire racks; cool completely.

5. Tint portions of white frosting with assorted food colorings. Spread desired colors of frosting over cookies. Decorate as desired.

Butterfly Cookies

Cookie Pops

Makes 20 cookies

> **1 package (20 ounces) refrigerated sugar cookie dough**
> **All-purpose flour (optional)**
> **20 (4-inch) lollipop sticks**
> **Assorted frostings, glazes and decors**

1. Preheat oven to 350°F. Grease cookie sheets.

2. Remove dough from wrapper according to package directions. Sprinkle with flour to minimize sticking, if necessary.

3. Cut dough in half. Reserve 1 half; refrigerate remaining dough. Roll reserved dough to ⅛-inch thickness. Cut out cookies using 3½-inch cookie cutters.

4. Place lollipop sticks on cookies so that tips of sticks are imbedded in cookies. Carefully turn cookies so sticks are in back; place on prepared cookie sheets. Repeat with remaining dough.

5. Bake 7 to 11 minutes or until edges are lightly browned. Cool cookies on cookie sheets 2 minutes. Remove cookies to wire racks; cool completely.

6. Decorate with frostings, glazes and decors as desired.

Reese's® Haystacks

Makes about 2 dozen treats

> **1⅔ cups (10-ounce package) REESE'S® Peanut Butter Chips**
> **1 tablespoon shortening (do *not* use butter, margarine, spread or oil)**
> **2½ cups (5-ounce can) chow mein noodles**

1. Line tray with wax paper.

2. Place peanut butter chips and shortening in medium microwave-safe bowl. Microwave at HIGH (100%) 1 minute; stir. If necessary, microwave at HIGH an additional 15 seconds at a time, stirring after each heating, just until chips are melted and mixture is smooth when stirred. Immediately add chow mein noodles; stir to coat.

3. Drop mixture by heaping teaspoons onto prepared tray or into paper candy cups. Let stand until firm. If necessary, cover and refrigerate several minutes until firm. Store in tightly covered container.

Cookie Pops

Smiley Oatmeal Cookies

Makes about 5 dozen cookies

COOKIES
1 Butter Flavor CRISCO® Stick or 1 cup Butter Flavor CRISCO® all-vegetable shortening
1 cup firmly packed light brown sugar
¾ cup granulated sugar
2 eggs
1 teaspoon vanilla
2½ cups all-purpose flour
1 teaspoon baking soda
½ teaspoon salt
1 cup oats (quick or old-fashioned, uncooked)
1 cup flake coconut

FROSTING
2 cups confectioners' sugar
¼ Butter Flavor CRISCO® Stick or ¼ cup Butter Flavor CRISCO® all-vegetable shortening
5 to 6 teaspoons milk

DECORATION
Peanut butter candy pieces
Red licorice laces

1. Heat oven to 350°F. Place sheets of foil on countertop for cooling cookies. For cookies, combine 1 cup shortening, brown sugar, granulated sugar, eggs and vanilla in large bowl. Beat at medium speed of electric mixer until well blended.

2. Combine flour, baking soda and salt. Add gradually to creamed mixture at low speed. Beat until well blended. Stir in oats and coconut with spoon. Shape tablespoonfuls of dough into 1-inch balls. Place 2 inches apart on ungreased baking sheet.

3. Bake at 350°F for 8 to 10 minutes or until very light brown and set. *Do not overbake.* Flatten slightly with spatula to level tops. Cool 2 minutes on baking sheet. Remove cookies to foil to cool completely.

4. For frosting, combine confectioners' sugar, ¼ cup shortening and milk in medium bowl. Beat at low speed until well blended and creamy. Spread thin layer on cookies. Decorate before frosting sets.

5. For decoration, make faces on cookies by placing candy pieces for eyes. Cut licorice into short strips. Form into different shapes for mouths. Press into frosting.

Smiley Oatmeal Cookies

Dino-Mite Dinosaurs

Makes 2 dozen cookies

1 cup (2 sticks) butter, softened
1¼ cups granulated sugar
1 large egg
2 squares (1 ounce each) semi-sweet chocolate, melted
½ teaspoon vanilla extract
2⅓ cups all-purpose flour
1 teaspoon baking powder
¼ teaspoon salt
1 cup white frosting
Assorted food colorings
1 cup "M&M's"® Chocolate Mini Baking Bits

In large bowl cream butter and sugar until light and fluffy; beat in egg, chocolate and vanilla. In medium bowl combine flour, baking powder and salt; add to creamed mixture. Wrap and refrigerate dough 2 to 3 hours.

Preheat oven to 350°F. Working with half the dough at a time on lightly floured surface, roll to ¼-inch thickness. Cut into dinosaur shapes using 4-inch cookie cutters. Place about 2 inches apart on ungreased cookie sheets. Bake 10 to 12 minutes. Cool 2 minutes on cookie sheets; cool completely on wire racks.

Tint frosting desired colors. Frost cookies and decorate with "M&M's"® Chocolate Mini Baking Bits. Store in tightly covered container.

Dino-Mite Dinosaurs

Peanut Butter Chips and Jelly Bars

Makes about 16 bars

1½ **cups all-purpose flour**
½ **cup sugar**
¾ **teaspoon baking powder**
½ **cup (1 stick) cold butter or margarine**
1 **egg, beaten**
¾ **cup grape jelly**
1⅔ **cups (10-ounce package) REESE'S® Peanut Butter Chips, divided**

1. Heat oven to 375°F. Grease 9-inch square baking pan.

2. Stir together flour, sugar and baking powder in large bowl. With pastry blender or two knives, cut in butter until mixture resembles coarse crumbs. Add egg; blend well. Reserve 1 cup mixture; press remaining mixture onto bottom of prepared pan. Stir jelly to soften; spread evenly over crust. Sprinkle 1 cup peanut butter chips over jelly. Stir together reserved crumb mixture with remaining ⅔ cup chips; sprinkle over top.

3. Bake 25 to 30 minutes or until lightly browned. Cool completely in pan on wire rack. Cut into bars.

Tip: For a whimsical twist on this tried-and-true classic, use cookie cutters to cut out shapes for added fun.

Rainbows

Makes about 5 dozen cookies

2¼ cups all-purpose flour
¼ teaspoon salt
1 cup sugar
¾ cup butter, softened
1 egg
1 teaspoon vanilla
1 teaspoon almond extract
Red, green, yellow and blue paste food coloring
White frosting and edible gold glitter dust

1. Combine flour and salt. Beat sugar and butter in large bowl at medium speed of electric mixer until fluffy. Beat in egg, vanilla and almond extract. Gradually add flour mixture. Beat at low speed until well blended. Divide dough into 10 equal sections.

2. Blend 4 sections dough and red food coloring, 3 sections dough and green food coloring and 2 sections dough and yellow food coloring and remaining dough and blue food coloring. Wrap each section in plastic wrap. Refrigerate 30 minutes.

3. Shape blue dough into 8-inch log. Shape yellow dough into 8×3-inch rectangle; place on waxed paper. Place blue log in center of yellow rectangle. Fold yellow edges up and around blue log, pinching to seal. Roll to form smooth log.

4. Roll green dough into 8×5-inch rectangle on waxed paper. Place yellow log in center of green rectangle. Fold green edges up and around yellow log. Pinch to seal. Roll gently to form smooth log.

5. Roll red dough into 8×7-inch rectangle. Place green log in center of red rectangle. Fold red edges up and around green log. Pinch to seal. Roll gently to form smooth log. Wrap in plastic wrap; refrigerate 1 hour.

6. Preheat oven to 350°F. Grease cookie sheets. Cut log in half lengthwise. Cut each half into ¼-inch-thick slices. Place slices 1 inch apart on prepared cookie sheets. Bake 8 to 12 minutes. *(Do not brown.)* Cool on cookie sheets 1 minute. Remove to wire racks; cool completely.

7. Pipe small amount of frosting on bottom corner of 1 side of each cookie and sprinkle with glitter dust. Let stand 1 hour or until frosting sets.

FUN & GAMES

Football Cake

Makes 12 to 16 servings

1 package DUNCAN HINES® Moist Deluxe® Devil's Food Cake Mix

Decorator Frosting
¾ cup confectioners' sugar
2 tablespoons shortening plus additional for greasing
1 tablespoon cold water
1 tablespoon non-dairy powdered creamer
¼ teaspoon vanilla extract
Dash salt
1 container DUNCAN HINES® Creamy Home-Style Chocolate Frosting

1. Preheat oven to 350°F. Grease and flour 10-inch round cake pan. Prepare cake following package directions for basic recipe. Bake at 350°F for 45 to 55 minutes or until toothpick inserted in center comes out clean.

2. For decorator frosting, combine confectioners' sugar, shortening, water, non-dairy powdered creamer, vanilla extract and salt in small bowl. Beat at medium speed with electric mixer 2 minutes. Add more confectioners' sugar to thicken or water to thin frosting as needed.

3. Cut 2-inch wide piece from center of cake; remove. Place halves together to create football shape. Spread chocolate frosting on sides and top of cake. Place basketweave tip in pastry bag. Fill with decorator frosting. Make white frosting laces on football.

Tip: If a 10-inch round pan is not available, make 2 football cakes by following package directions for baking with two 9-inch cake pans.

50

Football Cake

Cookie Canvases

Makes 8 to 10 cookie canvases

1 package (20 ounces) refrigerated cookie dough, any flavor
All-purpose flour (optional)
Cookie Glaze (recipe follows)
Assorted liquid food colorings

Supplies
1 (3½-inch) square cardboard template
1 (2½×4½-inch) rectangular cardboard template
Small, clean craft paintbrushes

1. Preheat oven to 350°F. Grease cookie sheets.

2. Remove dough from wrapper according to package directions. Cut dough in half. Wrap half of dough in plastic wrap and refrigerate.

3. Roll remaining dough on floured surface to ¼-inch thickness. Sprinkle with flour to minimize sticking, if necessary. Cut out cookie shapes using cardboard templates as guides. Place cookies 2 inches apart on prepared cookie sheets. Repeat steps with remaining dough.

4. Bake 8 to 10 minutes or until edges are lightly browned. Remove from oven and straighten cookie edges with spatula. Cool cookies completely on cookie sheets. Prepare Cookie Glaze.

5. Place cookies on wire racks set over waxed paper. Drizzle Cookie Glaze over cookies. Let stand at room temperature 40 minutes or until glaze is set. Place food colors in small bowls. Using small, clean craft paintbrushes, decorate cookies with food colorings by "painting" designs such as rainbows, flowers and animals.

Cookie Glaze: Combine 4 cups powdered sugar and 4 tablespoons milk in a small bowl. Stir; add 1 to 2 tablespoons more milk as needed to make a medium-thick, pourable glaze.

Cookie Canvases

Chocolate X and O Cookies

Makes about 5 dozen cookies

⅔ cup butter or margarine, softened
1 cup sugar
2 teaspoons vanilla extract
2 eggs
2 tablespoons light corn syrup
2½ cups all-purpose flour
½ cup HERSHEY'S Cocoa
½ teaspoon baking soda
¼ teaspoon salt
Decorating icing

1. Beat butter, sugar and vanilla in large bowl on medium speed of mixer until fluffy. Add eggs; beat well. Beat in corn syrup.

2. Combine flour, cocoa, baking soda and salt; gradually add to butter mixture, beating until well blended. Cover; refrigerate until dough is firm enough to handle.

3. Heat oven to 350°F. Shape dough into X and O shapes.* Place on ungreased cookie sheet.

4. Bake 5 minutes or until set. Remove from cookie sheet to wire rack. Cool completely. Decorate as desired with icing.

To shape X's: Shape rounded teaspoons of dough into 3-inch logs. Place 1 log on cookie sheet; press lightly in center. Place another 3-inch log on top of first one, forming X shape. To shape O's: Shape rounded teaspoon dough into 5-inch logs. Connect ends, pressing lightly, forming O shape.

Chocolate X and O Cookies

Mice Creams

Makes 6 servings

  1 pint vanilla ice cream
  1 (4-ounce) package READY CRUST® Mini-Graham Cracker Pie Crusts
  Ears—12 KEEBLER® Grasshopper® cookies
  Tails—3 chocolate twigs, broken in half *or* 6 (3-inch) pieces black shoestring licorice
  Eyes and noses—18 brown candy-coated chocolate candies
  Whiskers—2 teaspoons chocolate sprinkles

1. Place 1 scoop vanilla ice cream into each crust. Press cookie ears and tails into ice cream. Press eyes, noses, and whiskers in place. Serve immediately. Do not refreeze.

Prep Time: *15 minutes*

Touchdown Brownie Cups

Makes about 17 cupcakes

  1 cup (2 sticks) butter or margarine
  ½ cup HERSHEY'S Cocoa or HERSHEY'S Dutch Processed Cocoa
  1 cup packed light brown sugar
  ½ cup granulated sugar
  3 eggs
  1 teaspoon vanilla extract
  1 cup all-purpose flour
  1⅓ cups chopped pecans, divided

1. Heat oven to 350°F. Line 2½-inch muffin cups with paper or foil bake cups.

2. Place butter in large microwave-safe bowl; cover. Microwave at HIGH (100%) 1½ minutes or until melted. Add cocoa; stir until smooth. Add brown sugar and granulated sugar; stir until well blended. Add eggs and vanilla; beat well. Add flour and 1 cup pecans; stir until well blended. Fill prepared muffin cups about ¾ full with batter; sprinkle about 1 teaspoon remaining pecans over top of each.

3. Bake 20 to 25 minutes or until tops are beginning to dry and crack. Cool completely in cups on wire rack.

Mice Creams

Play Ball

Makes 24 cupcakes

    2 cups plus 1 tablespoon all-purpose flour, divided
    ¾ cup granulated sugar
    ¾ cup packed brown sugar
    1 tablespoon baking powder
    1 teaspoon salt
    ½ teaspoon baking soda
    1¼ cups milk
    ½ cup shortening
    3 eggs
    1½ teaspoons vanilla
    ½ cup mini semisweet chocolate chips
    1 container (16 ounces) vanilla frosting
    Assorted candies and food colorings

1. Preheat oven to 350°F. Line 24 regular-size (2½-inch) muffin pan cups with paper baking cups.

2. Combine 2 cups flour, sugars, baking powder, salt and baking soda in medium bowl. Beat milk, shortening, eggs and vanilla in large bowl with electric mixer at medium speed until well combined. Add flour mixture; blend well. Beat at high speed 3 minutes, scraping side of bowl frequently. Toss mini chocolate chips with remaining 1 tablespoon flour; stir into batter. Divide evenly among prepared muffin cups.

3. Bake 20 minutes or until toothpick inserted into centers comes out clean. Cool in pan on wire racks 5 minutes. Remove cupcakes to racks; cool completely. Decorate with desired frostings and candies as shown in photo.

Picasso's Palette

Makes 10 to 12 servings

1 (9-inch) round cake
1 (10-inch) round cake board, covered, or large plate
1 cup prepared white frosting
Assorted color decorator gels
Red pull-apart licorice twist
1 pretzel rod

1. Trim top and side of cake. Cut out small circle on one side of cake; cut piece from side of cake to create palette shape as shown in photo. Place on prepared cake board.

2. Tint frosting light brown.

3. Frost entire cake with brown frosting.

4. Pipe spots of paint on palette with decorator gels.

5. Create artist's paintbrush by cutting 2-inch lengths of licorice and attaching them to pretzel rod with foil.

Flapjack Party Stack

Makes 12 servings

1 package (18 ounces) yellow cake mix, plus ingredients to prepare mix
1 container (16 ounces) vanilla frosting
1 quart fresh strawberries, washed, hulled and sliced
1 cup caramel or butterscotch ice cream topping

1. Preheat oven to 350°F. Grease bottom and sides of 4 (9-inch) round cake pans with cooking spray; line bottoms with wax paper. Prepare cake according to package directions. Remove from oven and let cool in pans 15 minutes. Remove from pans and let cool completely on wire racks.

2. Place 1 cake layer on serving plate and frost top only with frosting swirls resembling whipped butter. Add a layer of sliced strawberries. Repeat with next 2 cake layers. Top stack with remaining layer. Pile frosting in center and add more strawberries.

3. Warm caramel topping in microwave just until pourable. Drizzle generous amount over stack of cake layers and berries, to resemble syrup on a stack of pancakes.

Picasso's Palette

nessie

Makes 24 to 28 servings

2 (10-inch) bundt cakes
2½ cups prepared white frosting
1 (40×20-inch) cake board, covered
Gumballs, assorted candies and red licorice twist

1. Cut one bundt cake in half. Cut second Bundt cake in quarters; set aside two quarters for another use.

2. Tint frosting light purple.

3. Frost two bundt cake halves with frosting, covering all sides of cake except two cut surfaces on each half. Frost two bundt cake quarters with frosting, covering all sides of cake except one cut surface on each quarter.

4. Stand two bundt cake halves on their cut surfaces, positioning them end to end in center of prepared cake board. Place bundt cake quarters, unfrosted cut surfaces down, on either side of bundt cake halves to resemble Loch Ness monster's head and tail as shown in photo.

5. Decorate monster with gumballs, assorted candies and licorice as shown in photo.

Mini Pizza Cookies

Makes 8 cookies

1 20-ounce tube of refrigerated sugar cookie dough
2 cups (16 ounces) prepared pink frosting
"M&M's"® Chocolate Mini Baking Bits
Variety of additional toppings such as shredded coconut, granola, raisins, nuts, small pretzels, snack mixes, sunflower seeds, popped corn and mini marshmallows

Preheat oven to 350°F. Lightly grease cookie sheets; set aside. Divide dough into 8 equal portions. On lightly floured surface, roll each portion of dough into ¼-inch-thick circle; place about 2 inches apart onto prepared cookie sheets. Bake 10 to 13 minutes or until golden brown on edges. Cool completely on wire racks. Spread top of each pizza with frosting; sprinkle with "M&M's"® Chocolate Mini Baking Bits and 2 or 3 suggested toppings.

TREATS & SWEETS

Surprise Package Cupcakes

Makes 24 cupcakes

  1 package (18 ounces) chocolate cake mix, plus ingredients to prepare mix
  1 container (16 ounces) vanilla frosting
     Food coloring (optional)
  1 tube (4¼ ounces) white decorator icing
 72 chewy fruit squares, assorted colors
     Assorted round sprinkles and birthday candles

1. Line standard (2½-inch) muffin cups with paper liners, or spray with nonstick cooking spray. Prepare cake and bake in muffin cups according to directions. Cool in pans on wire racks 15 minutes. Remove cupcakes and cool completely.

2. If desired, tint frosting with food coloring, adding a few drops at a time until desired color is reached. Frost cupcakes with white or tinted frosting.

3. Use decorator icing to pipe "ribbons" on fruit squares to resemble wrapped presents. Place 3 candy presents on each cupcake. Decorate with sprinkles and candles as desired.

Surprise Package Cupcakes

Cranberry Gorp

Makes 20 servings

- ¼ cup unsalted butter
- ¼ cup packed light brown sugar
- 1 tablespoon maple syrup
- 1 teaspoon curry powder
- ½ teaspoon ground cinnamon
- 1½ cups dried cranberries
- 1½ cups coarsely chopped walnuts and/or slivered almonds
- 1½ cups lightly salted pretzel nuggets

1. Preheat oven to 300°F. Grease 15×10-inch jelly-roll pan. Combine butter, brown sugar and maple syrup in large saucepan; heat over medium heat until butter is melted. Stir in curry powder and cinnamon. Add cranberries, walnuts and pretzels; stir to combine.

2. Spread mixture on prepared pan. Bake 15 minutes or until mixture is crunchy and light brown.

Creamy Strawberry-Orange Pops

Makes 6 servings

- 1 container (8 ounces) strawberry-flavored yogurt
- ¾ cup orange juice
- 2 teaspoons vanilla
- 2 cups frozen whole strawberries
- 2 teaspoons sugar
- 6 (7-ounce) paper cups
- 6 wooden sticks

1. Combine yogurt, orange juice and vanilla in food processor or blender. Cover and blend until smooth.

2. Add frozen strawberries and sugar. Blend until smooth. Pour into 6 paper cups, filling each about ¾ full. Place in freezer for 1 hour. Insert wooden stick into center of each. Freeze completely. Peel cup off each pop to serve.

Cranberry Gorp

Peanut Butter Ice Cream Triangles

Makes about 10 ice cream sandwiches

1½ cups all-purpose flour
½ teaspoon baking powder
½ teaspoon baking soda
¼ teaspoon salt
½ cup butter, softened
½ cup granulated sugar
½ cup packed brown sugar
½ cup creamy peanut butter
1 egg
1 teaspoon vanilla
2½ to 3 cups vanilla, cinnamon or chocolate ice cream, softened

1. Preheat oven to 350°F. Grease cookie sheets.

2. Combine flour, baking powder, baking soda and salt in small bowl; set aside. Beat butter, granulated sugar and brown sugar in large bowl of electric mixer at medium speed until light and fluffy. Beat in peanut butter, egg and vanilla until well blended. Gradually beat in flour mixture on low speed until blended.

3. Divide dough in half. Roll each piece of dough between 2 sheets of waxed paper or plastic wrap into 10×10-inch square, about ⅛ inch thick. Remove top sheet of waxed paper; invert dough onto prepared cookie sheet. Remove second sheet of waxed paper.

4. Score dough into four 4-inch squares. Score each square diagonally into two triangles. *Do not cut completely through dough.* Repeat with remaining dough. Combine excess scraps of dough; roll out and score into additional triangles.

5. Bake 12 to 13 minutes or until set and edges are golden brown. Cool cookies 2 minutes on cookie sheets. Cut through score marks with knife; cool completely on cookie sheets.

6. Place half the cookies on flat surface. Spread ¼ to ⅓ cup softened ice cream on flat side of each cookie; top with remaining cookies. Wrap in plastic wrap and freeze 1 hour or up to 2 days.

Peanut Butter Ice Cream Triangle

Sweet Treat Tortillas

Makes 6 servings

> 4 (7- to 8-inch) flour tortillas
> 4 ounces Neufchatel cheese, softened
> ¼ cup strawberry or other flavor spreadable fruit or preserves
> 1 medium banana, peeled and chopped

1. Spread each tortilla with 1 ounce Neufchatel cheese and 1 tablespoon spreadable fruit; top with ¼ of the banana.

2. Roll up tortillas; cut crosswise into thirds.

More Sweet Treats: Substitute your favorite chopped fruit for banana.

Cinnamon-Spice Treats: Omit spreadable fruit and banana. Mix small amounts of sugar, ground cinnamon and nutmeg into Neufchatel cheese; spread evenly onto tortillas. Sprinkle lightly with desired amount of chopped pecans or walnuts. Top with chopped fruit, if desired; roll up. Cut crosswise into thirds.

Chocolate Peanut Butter Cups

Makes 30 servings

> 1 package DUNCAN HINES® Moist Deluxe® Swiss Chocolate Cake Mix
> 1 container DUNCAN HINES® Creamy Home-Style Classic Vanilla Frosting
> ½ cup creamy peanut butter
> 15 miniature peanut butter cup candies, wrappers removed, cut in half vertically

1. Preheat oven to 350°F. Place 30 (2½-inch) paper liners in muffin cups.

2. Prepare, bake and cool cupcakes following package directions for basic recipe.

3. Combine vanilla frosting and peanut butter in medium bowl. Stir until smooth. Frost one cupcake. Decorate with peanut butter cup candy, cut side down. Repeat with remaining cupcakes, frosting and candies.

Tip: You may substitute Duncan Hines® Moist Deluxe® Devil's Food, Dark Chocolate Fudge or Butter Recipe Fudge Cake Mix flavors for Swiss Chocolate Cake Mix.

Sweet Treat Tortillas

Bamboozlers

Makes 1 dozen brownies

- **1 cup all-purpose flour**
- **¾ cup packed light brown sugar**
- **¼ cup unsweetened cocoa powder**
- **1 egg**
- **2 egg whites**
- **5 tablespoons margarine, melted**
- **¼ cup fat-free (skim) milk**
- **¼ cup honey**
- **1 teaspoon vanilla**
- **2 tablespoons semisweet chocolate chips**
- **2 tablespoons coarsely chopped walnuts**
- **Powdered sugar (optional)**

1. Preheat oven to 350°F. Grease and flour 8-inch square baking pan; set aside.

2. Combine flour, brown sugar and cocoa in medium bowl. Blend together egg, egg whites, margarine, milk, honey and vanilla in medium bowl. Add to flour mixture; mix well. Pour into prepared baking pan; sprinkle with chocolate chips and walnuts.

3. Bake brownies until they spring back when lightly touched in center, about 30 minutes. Cool completely in pan on wire rack. Sprinkle with powdered sugar just before serving, if desired.

Peanutters: Substitute peanut butter chips for chocolate chips and peanuts for walnuts.

Butterscotch Babies: Substitute butterscotch chips for chocolate chips and pecans for walnuts.

Brownie Sundaes: Serve brownies on dessert plates. Top each brownie with a scoop of vanilla nonfat frozen yogurt and 2 tablespoons nonfat chocolate or caramel sauce.

Bamboozlers

Peanut Butter and Chocolate Spirals

Makes 4 dozen cookies

- 1 package (20 ounces) refrigerated sugar cookie dough
- 1 package (20 ounces) refrigerated peanut butter cookie dough
- ¼ cup unsweetened cocoa powder
- ⅓ cup peanut butter-flavored chips, chopped
- ¼ cup all-purpose flour
- ⅓ cup miniature chocolate chips

1. Remove each dough from wrapper according to package directions.

2. Place sugar cookie dough and cocoa in large bowl; mix with fork to blend. Stir in peanut butter chips.

3. Place peanut butter cookie dough and flour in another large bowl; mix with fork to blend. Stir in chocolate chips. Divide each dough in half; cover and refrigerate 1 hour.

4. Roll each dough on floured surface to 12×6-inch rectangle. Layer each half of peanut butter dough onto each half of chocolate dough. Roll up doughs, starting at long end to form 2 (12-inch) rolls. Wrap in plastic wrap; refrigerate 1 hour.

5. Preheat oven to 375°F. Cut dough into ½-inch-thick slices. Place cookies 2 inches apart on ungreased cookie sheets.

6. Bake 10 to 12 minutes or until lightly browned. Remove to wire racks; cool completely.

Peanut Butter and Chocolate Spirals

Soft Pretzels

Makes 8 servings

**1 package (16 ounces) hot roll mix plus ingredients
    to prepare mix**
1 egg white
2 teaspoons water
**2 tablespoons *each* assorted coatings: coarse salt,
    sesame seeds, poppy seeds, dried oregano leaves**

1. Prepare hot roll mix according to package directions.

2. Preheat oven to 375°F. Spray baking sheets with nonstick cooking spray; set aside.

3. Divide dough equally into 16 pieces; roll each piece with hands to form rope, 7 to 10 inches long. Place on prepared cookie sheets; form into desired shape (hearts, wreaths, pretzels, snails, loops, etc.).

4. Beat egg white and water in small bowl until foamy. Brush onto dough shapes; sprinkle each shape with 1½ teaspoons of one coating.

5. Bake until golden brown, about 15 minutes. Serve warm or at room temperature.

Fruit Twists: Omit coatings. Prepare dough and roll into ropes as directed. Place ropes on lightly floured surface. Roll out, or pat, each rope into rectangle, ¼ inch thick; brush each rectangle with about 1 teaspoon spreadable fruit or preserves. Fold each rectangle lengthwise in half; twist into desired shape. Bake as directed.

Cheese Twists: Omit coatings. Prepare dough and roll into ropes as directed. Place ropes on lightly floured surface. Roll out, or pat, each rope into rectangle, ¼ inch thick. Sprinkle each rectangle with about 1 tablespoon shredded Cheddar or other flavor cheese. Fold each rectangle lengthwise in half; twist into desired shape. Bake as directed.

Soft Pretzels

LET THEM EAT CAKE!

Brownie Sundae Cake

Makes 12 slices

1 (19- to 21-ounce) package fudge brownie mix, prepared according to package directions for cake-like brownies
1 cup "M&M's"® Semi-Sweet Chocolate Mini Baking Bits
½ cup chopped nuts, optional
1 quart vanilla ice cream, softened
¼ cup caramel or butterscotch ice cream topping

Line 2 (9-inch) round cake pans with aluminum foil, extending slightly over edges of pans. Lightly spray bottoms with vegetable cooking spray; set aside. Preheat oven as brownie mix package directs. Divide brownie batter evenly between pans; sprinkle ½ cup "M&M's"® Semi-Sweet Chocolate Mini Baking Bits and ¼ cup nuts, if desired, over each pan. Bake 23 to 25 minutes or until edges begin to pull away from sides of pan. Cool completely. Remove layers by lifting foil from pans.

To assemble cake, place one brownie layer, topping-side down, in 9-inch springform pan. Carefully spread ice cream over brownie layer; drizzle with ice cream topping. Place second brownie layer on top of ice cream layer, topping-side up; press down lightly. Wrap in plastic wrap and freeze until firm. Remove from freezer about 15 minutes before serving. Remove side of pan. Cut into wedges.

Brownie Sundae Cake

Strawberry Shortcake

Makes 12 servings

Cake
   1 package DUNCAN HINES® Moist Deluxe® French Vanilla
      Cake Mix
   3 eggs
1¼ cups water
   ½ cup butter or margarine, softened

Filling and Topping
   2 cups whipping cream, chilled
   ⅓ cup sugar
   ½ teaspoon vanilla extract
   1 quart fresh strawberries, rinsed, drained and sliced
      Mint leaves for garnish

1. Preheat oven to 350°F. Grease two 9-inch round cake pans with butter or margarine. Sprinkle bottom and sides with granulated sugar.

2. For cake, combine cake mix, eggs, water and butter in large bowl. Beat at low speed with electric mixer until moistened. Beat at medium speed for 2 minutes. Pour into prepared pans. Bake at 350°F for 30 to 35 minutes or until toothpick inserted in center comes out clean. Cool in pan 10 minutes. Invert onto cooling rack. Cool completely.

3. For filling and topping, place whipping cream, sugar and vanilla extract in large bowl. Beat with electric mixer on high speed until stiff peaks form. Reserve ⅓ cup for garnish. Place one cake layer on serving plate. Spread with half of whipped cream and half of sliced strawberries. Place second layer on top of strawberries. Spread with remaining whipping cream and top with remaining strawberries. Dollop with reserved ½ cup whipped cream and garnish with mint leaves. Refrigerate until ready to serve.

Strawberry Shortcake

Birthday Extravaganza
Makes 12 to 14 servings

Cakes & Frosting
　　2 (9-inch) round cake layers
　　1 recipe Creamy White Frosting (recipe follows)

Decorations & Equipment
　　1 (10-inch) round cake board, covered
　　　　Assorted candies
　　　　Cooky Pops (page 42)
　　　　Rainbows (page 49)
　　1 Decorating bag, tip number 31

1. Trim tops of cakes. Place one cake layer on cake board. Frost top with about ½ cup Creamy White Frosting. Place second cake on top. Frost with Creamy White Frosting, reserving 1¼ cups for boarders.

2. Sprinkle candies on cake top to resemble confetti. Place Cookie Pops and Rainbows on top of cake.

3. Place remaining 1¼ cups Creamy White Frosting in decorating bag fitted with number 31 tip. To pipe shell border, hold bag at 45° angle just above cake edge at top. Squeeze until small mound is formed for base of shell, lifting slightly. Continue squeezing while pulling tip away from base until desired length. Stop squeezing; lift tip. Position tip almost touching tail of first shell. Repeat technique, completing top and bottom borders. Place candies between shells on bottom border.

For Cookie Pops, use teddy bear, candle, present and balloon cookie cutters. If not available, cut out squares for presents and circles for balloons.

Creamy White Frosting
Makes enough to fill and frost 2 (8-inch) cake layers

　　½ cup vegetable shortening
　　6 cups sifted powdered sugar, divided
　　3 tablespoons milk
　　2 teaspoons clear vanilla extract
　　　Additional milk as needed

Beat shortening in large bowl with electric mixer at medium speed until fluffy. Gradually beat in 3 cups sugar until well blended and smooth. Carefully beat in 3 tablespoons milk and vanilla. Gradually beat in remaining 3 cups sugar, adding more milk, 1 teaspoon at a time, as needed for good spreading consistency. Store in refrigerator.

Caramel Apple Cupcakes

Makes 24 cupcakes

1 package butter-recipe yellow cake mix plus ingredients to prepare
1 cup chopped dried apples
Caramel Frosting (recipe follows)
Chopped nuts (optional)

1. Preheat oven to 375°F. Line 24 regular-size (2½-inch) muffin pan cups with paper baking cups.

2. Prepare cake mix according to package directions. Stir in apples. Spoon batter into prepared muffin cups.

3. Bake 15 to 20 minutes or until toothpick inserted into centers comes out clean. Cool in pans on wire racks 10 minutes. Remove to racks; cool completely.

4. Prepare Caramel Frosting. Frost cupcakes. Sprinkle cupcakes with nuts, if desired.

Caramel Frosting

3 tablespoons butter
1 cup packed brown sugar
½ cup evaporated milk
⅛ teaspoon salt
3¾ cups powdered sugar
¾ teaspoon vanilla

1. Melt butter in 2-quart saucepan. Stir in brown sugar, evaporated milk and salt. Bring to a boil, stirring constantly. Remove from heat; cool to lukewarm.

2. Beat in powdered sugar until frosting is of spreading consistency. Blend in vanilla.

Pineapple Upside-Down Cake

Makes 16 to 20 servings

Topping

    ½ cup butter or margarine
    1 cup firmly packed brown sugar
    1 can (20 ounces) pineapple slices, well drained
       Maraschino cherries, drained and halved
       Walnut halves

Cake

    1 package DUNCAN HINES® Moist Deluxe® Pineapple Supreme
       Cake Mix
    1 package (4-serving size) vanilla-flavor instant pudding and
       pie filling mix
    4 eggs
    1 cup water
    ½ cup oil

1. Preheat oven to 350°F.

2. For topping, melt butter over low heat in 12-inch cast-iron skillet or skillet with oven-proof handle. Remove from heat. Stir in brown sugar. Spread to cover bottom of skillet. Arrange pineapple slices, maraschino cherries and walnut halves in skillet. Set aside.

3. For cake, combine cake mix, pudding mix, eggs, water and oil in large mixing bowl. Beat at medium speed with electric mixer for 2 minutes. Pour batter evenly over fruit in skillet. Bake at 350°F for 1 hour or until toothpick inserted in center comes out clean. Invert onto serving plate.

Tip: Cake can be made in a 13×9×2-inch pan. Bake at 350°F for 45 to 55 minutes or until toothpick inserted in center comes out clean. Cake is also delicious using Duncan Hines® Moist Deluxe® Yellow Cake Mix.

Pineapple Upside-Down Cake

Hot Fudge Pudding Cake

Makes about 8 servings

1¼ cups granulated sugar, divided
1 cup all-purpose flour
½ cup HERSHEY'S Cocoa, divided
2 teaspoons baking powder
¼ teaspoon salt
½ cup milk
⅓ cup butter or margarine, melted
1½ teaspoons vanilla extract
½ cup packed light brown sugar
1¼ cups hot water
Whipped topping

1. Heat oven to 350°F.

2. Stir together ¾ cup granulated sugar, flour, ¼ cup cocoa, baking powder and salt. Stir in milk, butter and vanilla; beat until smooth. Pour batter into ungreased 9-inch square baking pan. Stir together remaining ½ cup granulated sugar, brown sugar and remaining ¼ cup cocoa; sprinkle mixture evenly over batter. Pour hot water over top. Do not stir.

3. Bake 35 to 40 minutes or until center is almost set. Let stand 15 minutes; spoon into dessert dishes, spooning sauce from bottom of pan over top. Garnish with whipped topping.

Prep Time: *10 minutes*
Bake Time: *35 minutes*
Cool Time: *15 minutes*

Hot Fudge Pudding Cake

Cubcakes

Makes 24 cupcakes

> 1 package (18 ounces) chocolate cake mix, plus ingredients to prepare mix
> 1 container (16 ounces) chocolate frosting
> 1 package (5 ounces) chocolate nonpareils
> 72 red cinnamon candies
> Chocolate sprinkles
> 1 tube (0.6 ounce) black piping gel

1. Line standard (2½-inch) muffin cups with paper liners, or spray with nonstick cooking spray. Prepare cake and bake in muffin cups according to directions. Cool in pans on wire racks 15 minutes. Remove cupcakes and cool completely.

2. Frost cooled cupcakes with chocolate frosting. Use nonpareils to make ears and muzzle. Add red candies for eyes and nose. Sprinkle on chocolate sprinkles for fur. Use piping gel to place dots on eyes and to make mouth.

Snowy Owl Cupcakes

Makes 24 cupcakes

> 1 package (18 ounces) white cake mix, plus ingredients to prepare mix
> 1 container (16 ounces) vanilla frosting
> 2½ cups sweetened, shredded coconut
> 48 round gummy candies
> 24 chocolate-covered coffee beans or black jelly beans
> 1 tub (0.6 ounce) black piping gel

1. Line standard (2½-inch) muffin cups with paper liners, or spray with nonstick cooking spray. Prepare cake and bake in muffin cups according to directions. Cool in pans on wire racks 15 minutes. Remove cupcakes and cool completely.

2. Frost cupcakes with vanilla frosting. Sprinkle coconut over each cupcake, covering completely. Place 2 gummy candies on each cupcake for eyes. Add chocolate-covered coffee bean for beak. Use piping gel to dot eyes.

Cubcakes

Cookies 'n' Cream Cake

Makes 10 to 12 servings

- 1 package (about 18 ounces) white cake mix
- 1 package (4-serving size) instant white chocolate-flavored pudding and pie filling mix
- 1 cup vegetable oil
- 4 egg whites
- ½ cup milk
- 20 chocolate sandwich cookies, coarsely chopped
- ½ cup semisweet chocolate chips
- 1 teaspoon vegetable shortening
- 4 chocolate sandwich cookies, cut into quarters for garnish

1. Preheat oven to 350°F. Spray 10-inch fluted tube pan with nonstick cooking spray.

2. Beat cake mix, pudding mix, oil, egg whites and milk 2 minutes in large bowl with electric mixer at medium speed or until ingredients are well blended. Stir in chopped cookies; spread in prepared pan.

3. Bake 50 to 60 minutes or until cake springs back when lightly touched. Cool 1 hour in pan on wire rack. Invert cake onto serving plate; cool completely.

4. Combine chocolate chips and shortening in glass measuring cup. Heat in microwave at HIGH (100%) power 1 minute; stir. Continue heating at 15 second intervals, stirring, until melted and smooth. Drizzle glaze over cake and garnish with quartered cookies.

Cookies 'n' Cream Cake

ACKNOWLEDGMENTS

*T*he publisher would like to thank the companies and organizations listed below for the use of their recipes and photographs in this publication.

Duncan Hines® and Moist Deluxe® are registered trademarks of

Aurora Foods Inc.

Eagle Brand®

The Golden Grain Company®

Hebrew National®

Hershey Foods Corporation

Keebler® Company

© Mars, Incorporated 2004

Reckitt Benckiser Inc.

The J.M. Smucker Company

StarKist® Seafood Company

Washington Apple Commission

92

METRIC CONVERSION CHART

VOLUME MEASUREMENTS (dry)

1/8 teaspoon = 0.5 mL
1/4 teaspoon = 1 mL
1/2 teaspoon = 2 mL
3/4 teaspoon = 4 mL
1 teaspoon = 5 mL
1 tablespoon = 15 mL
2 tablespoons = 30 mL
1/4 cup = 60 mL
1/3 cup = 75 mL
1/2 cup = 125 mL
2/3 cup = 150 mL
3/4 cup = 175 mL
1 cup = 250 mL
2 cups = 1 pint = 500 mL
3 cups = 750 mL
4 cups = 1 quart = 1 L

VOLUME MEASUREMENTS (fluid)

1 fluid ounce (2 tablespoons) = 30 mL
4 fluid ounces (1/2 cup) = 125 mL
8 fluid ounces (1 cup) = 250 mL
12 fluid ounces (1 1/2 cups) = 375 mL
16 fluid ounces (2 cups) = 500 mL

WEIGHTS (mass)

1/2 ounce = 15 g
1 ounce = 30 g
3 ounces = 90 g
4 ounces = 120 g
8 ounces = 225 g
10 ounces = 285 g
12 ounces = 360 g
16 ounces = 1 pound = 450 g

DIMENSIONS

1/16 inch = 2 mm
1/8 inch = 3 mm
1/4 inch = 6 mm
1/2 inch = 1.5 cm
3/4 inch = 2 cm
1 inch = 2.5 cm

OVEN TEMPERATURES

250°F = 120°C
275°F = 140°C
300°F = 150°C
325°F = 160°C
350°F = 180°C
375°F = 190°C
400°F = 200°C
425°F = 220°C
450°F = 230°C

BAKING PAN SIZES

Utensil	Size in Inches/Quarts	Metric Volume	Size in Centimeters
Baking or Cake Pan (square or rectangular)	8 × 8 × 2	2 L	20 × 20 × 5
	9 × 9 × 2	2.5 L	23 × 23 × 5
	12 × 8 × 2	3 L	30 × 20 × 5
	13 × 9 × 2	3.5 L	33 × 23 × 5
Loaf Pan	8 × 4 × 3	1.5 L	20 × 10 × 7
	9 × 5 × 3	2 L	23 × 13 × 7
Round Layer Cake Pan	8 × 1½	1.2 L	20 × 4
	9 × 1½	1.5 L	23 × 4
Pie Plate	8 × 1¼	750 mL	20 × 3
	9 × 1¼	1 L	23 × 3
Baking Dish or Casserole	1 quart	1 L	—
	1½ quart	1.5 L	—
	2 quart	2 L	—